CELADINE

Charles Evered

BROADWAY PLAY PUBLISHING INC
New York
www.broadwayplaypublishing.com
info@broadwayplaypublishing.com

CELADINE
© Copyright 2005 by Charles Evered

Cover photo by T Charles Erickson
1st printing: December 2005
I S B N: 978-0-88145-283-9

Book design: Marie Donovan
Word processing: Microsoft Word
Typographic controls: Xerox Ventura Publisher 2.0 P E
Typeface: Palatino
Printed and bound in the U S A

CELADINE was given its world premiere production at The George Street Playhouse (Managing Director, Mitchell Krieger; Producing Director, George Ryan) in New Brunswick, New Jersey, opening 19 November 2004. The cast and creative contributors were:

MARY .... Leslie Lyles
ELLIOT .... Matt Pepper
CELADINE .... Amy Irving
JEFFREY .... Rob Eigenbrod
ROWLEY .... Michael Countryman

Director .... David Saint
Scenic design .... Michael Anania
Costume design .... David Murin
Lighting .... Joe Saint
Sound .... Christopher J Bailey

CHARACTERS & SETTING

CELADINE, *forties/fifties, proprietor of the house*
MARY, *forties/fifties,* CELADINE's *maid servant and friend*
JEFFREY, *a youth, mute*
ELLIOT, *a striking actor*
ROWLEY, *an unassuming man*

The play takes place in the Teale Coffeehouse, London, during the 1670's.

A note regarding music: Music in the style of mid-Baroque should be employed whenever appropriate, particularly during transitions.

for *my* Margaret

ACT ONE

(In the darkness, music. Then, at rise, the main room of a coffeehouse is revealed. It is not well kept. Knocking is heard and a man's voice [ELLIOT])

ELLIOT: Hello, inhabitants!? Hello! Hello! Is anyone present!? Hellooo!

(A woman, MARY, enters. She seems to have just woken up and has a hard lived beauty about her. She walks to the door, shouts at it)

MARY: Who dares knock at the crack of dawn?!

ELLIOT: Hark!? I warrant it is the "crack of noon," milady.

MARY: And what is that you say; "Hark!?" What *is* "Hark?"

ELLIOT: Only but a useful "term of art." You have my assurance.

MARY: I see. Then I would like to "Hark" as well: "Hark!"— do I detect the voice of an UN-interesting person?

ELLIOT: Why say you thus?

MARY: Because everyone interesting—is STILL ASLEEP! Now; tell me something interesting or I will go back to bed.

ELLIOT: Very well. *(Pause)* I—am an actor!

(She starts to walk away.)

MARY: Good day, sir.

ELLIOT: With—money!

(The woman stops. Goes back to the door)

MARY: You have money, you say?

ELLIOT: I do!

MARY: And you are an actor?

ELLIOT: That is correct!

MARY: Then you are a liar, sir. Good day.

(She starts to walk off again.)

ELLIOT: It is true, behold!

(Coins slide under the door. The woman stops, looks back at them. She walks over, picks them up and inspects them. After fixing her hair a little, she opens the door. A handsome man steps in. He is dressed in clothes that appear finer than they are. The woman regards him, then)

MARY: Your business, sir?

ELLIOT: This is the Teale Coffeehouse?

MARY: It is.

ELLIOT: Have you no customers?

MARY: Have you no vision?

ELLIOT: Do you know who I am?

MARY: Have you as yet identified yourself?

ELLIOT: Is it necessary that I must?

MARY: No sir, not at all. *(Pause)* Unless of course you want me to know who you are.

ELLIOT: Then you do *not* know?

MARY: Oh, but of course I do, sir.

ELLIOT: I naturally assumed you would.

MARY: You are the man I let in the house who keeps asking me whether I know him or not.

ELLIOT: But what of my features? The shape of my eyes, my chin? The familiar contour of my nose?

MARY: None provokes recognition, sir.

ELLIOT: Then what of this voice? No doubt you have heard this voice before?

MARY: I am afraid not, sir.

ELLIOT: Have you been to the theatre?

MARY: I have.

ELLIOT: Here in London?

MARY: Yes.

ELLIOT: And is your vision adequate?

MARY: My vision is fine, sir.

ELLIOT: Surely then you purchase seats far from the stage.

MARY: No sir. I sit up front.

ELLIOT: At the Drury Lane?

MARY: I do, sir.

ELLIOT: Then what of *The Plight of Zeus*? Did you not see that storied production?

MARY: I did see that production, sir. And who did you play?

ELLIOT: Zeus. The *title* character?

MARY: Oh. Oh, well—I do not have a great recollection, I am afraid. I do remember the production however.

ELLIOT: And your opinion of it?

MARY: I remember it as being—restful.

ELLIOT: "Restful?"

MARY: Yes. I recall the experience as being—fleeting in its entirety.

ELLIOT: "Fleeting?"

MARY: Aye, as though I had only to close my eyes— and when I opened them again three hours later, the entire experience had already passed. As though in—

ELLIOT: —a dream?

MARY: As good a word as any, sir.

ELLIOT: Then one would not be inaccurate in describing my performance as "encouraging of sleep?"

MARY: No sir, do not be so hard on your self. It did not "encourage" sleep as much as "facilitate" it.

ELLIOT: Yes, I thank you. That distinction does much to bolster my already acutely diminished self regard. Allow me to formally introduce myself: *(He extends his hand.)* Elliot Blakely: Actor, Tragedian.

MARY: Oh, yes, sir. Mary Maher: Harlot, Equestrian.

ELLIOT: What say you?

MARY: I jest, sir. I am allergic to horses. Now, as to your business?

ELLIOT: I am here for a play.

MARY: A play?

ELLIOT: Yes, I would like to order a play. Written for myself. This is the residence of the talented playwright and author Celadine, is it not?

MARY: At certain times.

ELLIOT: Do you act as her agent?

MARY: Among other things.

ELLIOT: Good. Then tell me: talk about town has it that she is "beside herself." Is that true?

MARY: Who else would she be "beside"—except herself?

ELLIOT: Is she capable of another play?

MARY: There is no one more capable. I will tell her you called.

(He bows ceremoniously.)

ELLIOT: Pleasant day.

MARY: I thank you kindly, sir.

(He exits. MARY closes the door behind him as suddenly we hear the sound of a woman, laughing. Bursting through the back door, on the shoulders of a handsome young man is CELADINE. She is laughing and whipping the young man playfully with her fan as he trots her around the room, stomping like a horse. MARY looks up in astonishment.)

MARY: What is this, milady?

CELADINE: Why, it is my new steed, Mary— have you no eyes?

MARY: Your new steed, eh? Might I have a go?

CELADINE: There will be time enough for that. First, let me "break him in" myself!

(They both laugh as the young man begins to slow down.)

CELADINE: There's a good horsy. Now, do put me down. Such a good horsy.

(The young man gently lowers her to the ground. She dismounts.)

MARY: You have been out all night.

CELADINE: Are you my mother now?

MARY: And where did you find your—mount?

CELADINE: Oh, he found me, the dear child. I broke the heel of my shoe and the sweet thing pounced out of nowhere and saved me, carrying me all the way across Saint James. Is he not a sight for sore eyes?

MARY: And for rested ones as well.

CELADINE: And do you know what I like about him best?

MARY: I can wager a guess—

CELADINE: —you would be wrong.

MARY: Then what?

CELADINE: He cannot speak.

MARY: Can he not?

CELADINE: No. And as a result, we have gotten along passing well. Which leads me to surmise that the problem with the other men I have known is that they could speak.

MARY: That has the sound of reason.

CELADINE: Go on, try to speak with him.

MARY: Very well.

(MARY *looks toward the young man, who smiles cheerfully.*)

MARY: Come hither, boy. (*He moves to her*) Tell me. Do you speak?

(*He motions toward his mouth, shrugging his shoulders.*)

MARY: Not at all?

(*He nods no.*)

MARY: Do you churn butter?

(*He nods yes.*)

MARY: And chop wood?

(*He nods yes.*)

MARY: And yet not a peep from you?

(He nods no.)

MARY *(To* CELADINE*)* I declare he is the perfect man.

CELADINE: I warrant we shall keep him.

MARY: But where?

CELADINE: Here, where else?

MARY: What will the neighbors say?

CELADINE: What they say already. Only now it will have a basis in fact. He goes by "Jeffrey."

MARY: How do you surmise?

CELADINE: I had him write it in the dirt. *(To* JEFFREY*)* Jeffrey, go to the kitchen and feed yourself.

(She claps twice as JEFFREY *promptly gallops into the kitchen like a horse.* MARY *turns to* CELADINE.*)*

MARY: You are reckless.

CELADINE: I am alive.

MARY: We can hardly afford to keep ourselves.

CELADINE: The poor thing has not eaten in days. And for your information: he cannot speak because he has no tongue.

MARY: No tongue? And how is that?

CELADINE: I heard a rumor—which of course means it is likely true—that as a boy of only fourteen—he spoke against his church so they cut out his tongue.

MARY: An evil act.

CELADINE: He can use shelter and we can use a strong back.

MARY: The strange reputation of this house will only increase.

CELADINE: If it is even possible.

MARY: Your kind heart will land us in debtors prison. We have a coffeehouse with no business and an increasingly odd roster of employees.

CELADINE: Put your trust in Providence.

MARY: I would, if Providence would see fit to pay our bills. You had two callers.

CELADINE: Did I?

MARY: One; an actor who wants a play.

CELADINE: I fear myself incapable.

MARY: We can make use of the money.

CELADINE: I am not much for worldly concerns of late.

MARY: When have you ever been?

CELADINE: I am going up to rest my eyes.

(She starts up the stairs)

MARY: You were seen, Celi.

(CELADINE stops.)

CELADINE: What is it you say?

MARY: You were seen—witnessed, in your—"attempt."

CELADINE: My "attempt."

MARY: At Westminster.

CELADINE: What is it you think you know?

MARY: That you made your way to the top, to the left spire. You walked out to the ledge and that if it were not for the bell ringer, Stephens—

CELADINE: —you lack understanding.

MARY: I understand a true friend would never—

CELADINE: —I was collecting air for my lungs.
I was out for a walk. No more. No less.

MARY: Do you regard me as ignorant?

CELADINE: You are the true dramatist, Mary.

MARY: And so I know nothing of the workings of your
heart?

CELADINE: You are as accurate regarding the intent
of my heart as critics have been regarding the intent of
my pen. And what if I had such a fanciful thought, eh?
You saw the sign. You yourself saw the candle go out.

MARY: Pray, no more of the candle.

CELADINE: You saw it as clearly as I. I held the candle.
It illuminated *her* face—the painting you made of her
face, and without even a breath of air, OUT it went.
Could that not be construed as a sign? She beckons me.

MARY: This is how rumors begin.

CELADINE: What "rumors?"

MARY: That you are losing your mind.

CELADINE: But what "rumor" is that? That is a fact!
I am but a ghost to myself.

MARY: You are no "ghost," only a self involved
coquette.

CELADINE: And you Mary are a simple and dull stone.

MARY: Children die.

CELADINE: What is that you say?

MARY: Children die.

CELADINE: Is that how we regard her now? Now she
is consigned to be known as nothing but a subject in a
sentence outlining a general statement of fact? Lumped

in altogether, just one in a line of any such "sad" occurrences—

MARY: —yes, except that we loved her.

CELADINE: By Heaven, "Loved her"? Is that all we did? Did you not raise her with me? Did she not curl herself against *your* breast as well as mine? Do you not recall the way the world collapsed into a tunnel of light when she would bless us with something as seemingly inconsequential as a *grin*? How we would have to catch our breath when she saw fit to reward us with a smile?

MARY: I remember, yes.

CELADINE: And her laugh? What of that, eh? Do you not recall how every care in the world fell off us— when it would wake us up in the morning? Her laughter was more profound than scripture. It danced around moons. It lit dark caverns. It leapt mountains and thrust spears of truth into cynical and blackened hearts and yet all you can do is "remember"?

MARY: I am not deserving of this.

(Pause)

CELADINE: Dear Mary—

MARY: ...someone else came.

CELADINE: Who?

MARY: "Rowley," I believe he called himself.

CELADINE: Did he?

MARY: Yes. He seemed to have the demeanor of a used horse salesman. Somewhat "shifty," I thought.

CELADINE: Was he alone?

MARY: Entirely.

CELADINE: And his message?

MARY: That he would call again.

(CELADINE *starts up, then stops again, looks down at* MARY.)

CELADINE: Your love for me—breaks my heart.

MARY: That is not my intention. My love is meant to repair it.

CELADINE: Such is my misfortune—for not being able to tell the difference.

(*Knocking is heard.* MARY *starts for the door*)

CELADINE: I will answer it. You make sure our friend has enough to eat.

MARY: Aye.

(CELADINE *walks over to her, kisses her sweetly on the cheek.*)

CELADINE: My sweet, Mary.

(MARY *smiles, goes into the kitchen.* CELADINE *turns to the door, shouts*)

CELADINE: Who knocks?!

(*A voice from the other side of the door.*)

VOICE: It is a friend, milady.

CELADINE: And *who* is my friend?

VOICE: Why, "the truth" milady. The truth is your friend.

CELADINE: Pray, why is the truth my friend?

VOICE: Because whether you believe it or not— it remains.

(*She slowly opens the door, then walks away from it. Stepping inside is an unassuming middle aged man with tufts of unkempt hair sprouting off his head. The man stops and regards her. She turns back at him.*)

CELADINE: "Rowley."

ROWLEY: At your service.

CELADINE: You have aged.

ROWLEY: You have not.

(He presents her with a pineapple he had hidden behind his back.)

CELADINE: What is this?

ROWLEY: It is called a "Pine Apple."

CELADINE: It is very odd.

ROWLEY: I have rather taken a liking to them. "Prickly on the outside, yet soft and sweet on the..."

CELADINE: —oh, do spare me your tired metaphors. Only stupid women in need of money would abide them.

ROWLEY: You have not changed.

CELADINE: State the purpose of your visit.

ROWLEY: If you ever loved me, it was only for who I could have been-not for who I was.

CELADINE: I was in love with you. For who you were.

ROWLEY: I failed you.

CELADINE: You failed yourself.

ROWLEY: You see, I cannot tell you how much I miss that. Being spoken to like that. No one insults me anymore. I cannot pay people to insult me. And I have!

CELADINE: Make a habit of telling your friends the truth. I promise—you will be insulted.

ROWLEY: I did see your latest play.

CELADINE: Did you?

ROWLEY: It was revolutionary.

CELADINE: Yes, revolutionary and un-attended.

ROWLEY: It can be said you do not write for the many-headed multitude.

CELADINE: Have you come here to state the obvious? Perhaps you would care to remind me that water is wet?

ROWLEY: Your work has more merit than that of Aphra Behn.

CELADINE: THAT is a name you would do well never to mention in my company again.

ROWLEY: But why? She is not half the writer you are. Anyone can write in accordance with people's wishes. It is more than whispered in several corners of only the most august literary salons that *you* dear lady, are the most brilliant writer in all of England.

CELADINE: Yes, and the least successful.

ROWLEY: Oh, but Miss Behn is only—sorry, "you know who," is more or less perceived as nothing but a literary facilitator, really.

CELADINE: She does write to taste, that is true. State your purpose or leave. I require sleep.

ROWLEY: There, see, *that!* Extraordinary. You want to take leave of me—*before* I make it clear I would like to take leave of you. No one does that to me anymore. I cannot tell you how much the pure audacity of that thrills me!

CELADINE: Shut the door behind you. (*She starts up the stairs.*)

ROWLEY: Your country—is in need of your service.

(*She turns back to him.*)

ROWLEY: The Dutch. An invasion is feared any day. Your skills of cunning are much in demand.

CELADINE: This is a worldly consideration I no longer find compelling.

ROWLEY: The matter is pressing, I can assure you.

CELADINE: Do you never think of her anymore? Does she never appear to you as she does to me? Do you ever hear her voice? Do you ever have a recollection even? You may not have raised her, but she was yours as well as mine.

ROWLEY: —as you might have imagined, I have been somewhat "otherwise engaged."

CELADINE: Go thy ways; out of my sight.

ROWLEY: What else would you have me say?

CELADINE: That you *recall* her! That in some corner of your being she still lives.

ROWLEY: Unlike you, I do not have the luxury of so frequently taking a dip in the inviting and medicinal waters of self pity.

(She grabs a candle holder off the table, threatens him with it.)

CELADINE: You do not get insulted enough? Is that your complaint? If you utter one more glib word— I will beat the repulsive smugness right out of you.

(He slowly manages to lower her hand)

ROWLEY: So you are as mad as they say.

CELADINE: It was you who put us on that ship.

ROWLEY: And so now I am Prospero—responsible for the weather as well?

CELADINE: I wish for you to die in a little way— like little men do. *(She starts up the stairs.)*

ROWLEY: I do not recall her. But not for the reasons you think. I do not recall her for my own self-preservation.

(He starts toward the door. She turns to him.)

CELADINE: Stop!

(He turns.)

CELADINE: I may—be inclined to help you. *(Pause)* But only for something in return.

ROWLEY: You will be paid.

CELADINE: Your money continues to hold little sway over me.

ROWLEY: Then what?

CELADINE: I want her raised from the dead.

ROWLEY: You are in ill humor.

CELADINE: In name, at least. I want her to have existed in name. I want her acknowledged—as your own.

ROWLEY: For reasons outside of my own control, that may not—

CELADINE: —then we have no business, goodnight.

(She starts up the stairs)

ROWLEY: Very well!

CELADINE: And you will swear on it?

ROWLEY: Yes. *(Pause)* Goodnight, Celadine.

CELADINE: Goodnight—good Rowley.

(He leaves. CELADINE stands frozen on the stairs as the lights fade to black with music.)

(Lights come up again the next day, as we see MARY standing over JEFFREY who is on his knees, drawing on the floor with a piece of charcoal.)

MARY: I cannot make it out. Try it again.

(He draws it again.)

MARY: Is it— a needle?

(He shakes his head "yes." He draws something else.)

MARY: A needle and—a snake?

(He lowers his shoulders, exasperated.)

MARY: Well, have patience you hunk of beef!

(CELADINE comes down the stairs.)

CELADINE: What are you two about?

MARY: He is trying to communicate his trade to me.

CELADINE: I thought he was a horse. Is that not trade enough?

MARY: As far as I can tell, he pricks the heads of snakes with needles. Is there such thing as a "snake prickler?"

(JEFFREY throws up his hands, giving up, as CELADINE casually glances at the drawing.)

CELADINE: He is a tailor.

(JEFFREY's face beams, he jumps up and down, shaking his head "yes," clapping and stomping like a horse again.)

MARY: How could you tell?

CELADINE: *(Pointing it out)* A needle and thread. Mary go fetch my sewing box, let us have a look at his form.

MARY: *(As JEFFREY bends to erase the drawing)* I am having a look at his form as we speak.

CELADINE: His *sewing* form!

(MARY goes and gets a sewing kit. CELADINE takes a seat in the middle of the room. MARY returns and hands the kit to her. CELADINE quickly threads a needle, turns to JEFFREY.)

CELADINE: Very well, stallion: *(She pulls up her dress.)* Get to work.

(JEFFREY stands motionless.)

MARY: Why that is forward, even for you.

CELADINE: On my undergarment. Do you not see the tear in the seam?

(JEFFREY *cautiously takes a peek at her undergarment. He sees the tear, then grabs the needle and thread from* CELADINE *and crawls partly under her dress. His "backside" and legs stick plainly out from the front of it.)*

CELADINE: That 'a boy, Jeffrey. Can you see down there?

(We see his head shake "yes" under her dress. A knock is heard.)

MARY: I will answer it.

(MARY opens the door. Stepping inside is ELLIOT*)*

MARY: *(To* CELADINE*)* It is the actor.

(ELLIOT turns toward CELADINE, *remaining behind her.)*

ELLIOT: Is that *the* Celadine!? Sage and literary flower!?

CELADINE: Pray, who carries on so?

ELLIOT: An admirer of your genius!

CELADINE: I see. In other words, someone who runs in very exclusive circles. Come closer. I wish not to crane my neck.

(ELLIOT walks in front of her. Starts to speak,

ELLIOT: Allow me to intro—

(He suddenly notices JEFFREY's *backside and legs sticking out from the front of her dress. He freezes.)*

CELADINE: Is something wrong?

ELLIOT: No, no—though perhaps this is not the best—

CELADINE: —do sit.

(ELLIOT sits. Awkward silence, then)

CELADINE: Your business?

ELLIOT: Yes, of course. Though I cannot help but notice there is a man under your dress.

CELADINE: A man? Oh, Jeffrey? Oh, do not pay him any mind. I have not had this done to me for the longest time.

ELLIOT: I am—sorry to hear that.

CELADINE: And as everyone knows, if holes such as this are not tended to on a regular basis, they have a tendency to—elongate.

ELLIOT: I—see. I myself am not a physician, but will take your—

CELADINE: —so, when a lady comes across someone willing to do this, especially a man, one can hardly pass up the opportunity.

ELLIOT: No, of course "one" could not.

MARY: *(Eager to join in)* Yes, usually, a woman is obliged to do this sort of thing for herself.

ELLIOT: Really? I imagine she would have to be a particularly *limber* woman.

CELADINE: What is that you say?

ELLIOT: Nothing. I had of course heard this was a "liberal" house—

CELADINE *(Toward her lap)* —Jeffrey, do come out and get some air. Meet Mister... Oh, I am very sorry—

ELLIOT: Blakely. Elliot Blakely, Thespian.

(JEFFREY *peeks out from under* CELADINE's *dress, shakes* ELLIOT's *hand)*

ELLIOT: Yes—very nice to—

(CELADINE *pushes* JEFFREY's *head back under her dress.)*

CELADINE: —back to work, Jeffrey.

(ELLIOT *stands, unable to take any more of it.*)

ELLIOT: I must say—

CELADINE: Sit!

(ELLIOT *sits as* MARY *struggles to contain her laughter.*)

CELADINE: There's a good Jeffrey—now finish me off!

(ELLIOT *stands.*)

ELLIOT: I really must protest—

CELADINE: Sit!

(ELLIOT *sits again as* JEFFREY *makes growling noises under her dress, trying to bite off the thread.*)

CELADINE: Oh, yes—yes Jeffrey, good boy!

(JEFFREY *breaks off the thread with his teeth.* CELADINE *reacts. As does* ELLIOT *and* MARY)

CELADINE: Yes! Well done, Jeffrey!

(JEFFREY *emerges from under* CELADINE's *dress, beaming with pride.*)

MARY: Yes, Jeffrey—if there is any chance you can do the same for me later, I would be most appreciative.

(JEFFREY *eagerly nods "yes".*)

CELADINE: Go feed him a carrot, will you Mary? He's been a good horsy.

MARY: Come, boy.

(MARY *leads a galloping* JEFFREY *off into the kitchen.* CELADINE *turns to* ELLIOT.)

CELADINE: You are a gullible fish. He was sewing my seam.

ELLIOT: Oh, well— Yes, of course.

CELADINE: Your business?

ELLIOT: I had hopes you might have a play for me.

CELADINE: You had false hopes. I have no play.

ELLIOT: Then, perhaps I could convince you to write one?

CELADINE: I am no longer inclined. You are wasting your time. Good day, sir. *(She starts upstairs.)*

ELLIOT: Is it true what they say?

(She turns back.)

CELADINE: If it would hurt me to hear it—then it must be.

ELLIOT: I saw your latest play.

CELADINE: Did you?

ELLIOT: Yes, opening night.

CELADINE: Otherwise known as "closing night."

ELLIOT: It was the silences between the words that I appreciated most.

CELADINE: I did not write those. The actors did. And as I recall, some of the buggers were quite prolific.

ELLIOT: Is it a habit of yours to repel compliments?

CELADINE: No, it is a habit of mine to repel happiness. Repulsed compliments are only a casualty of that larger policy. Good day, sir.

ELLIOT: Then I dare you to fend off the following barrage: You, Celadine, are brilliant! Your talent has no equal! You are an artist of the first order! Everyone in the know, knows this to be true. The reason your drama did not play a second night is because you are wholly out of touch with the spirit of your age. *That,* as everyone knows, is the sure sign of a great writer.

CELADINE: It may be sir, but more often than not,
it is the convenient justification— of a great failure.

ELLIOT: In your case however, it happens to be true.

CELADINE: I am without the ability to allow myself the
comfort of so delicious a delusion.

ELLIOT: Which only confirms the fact that in your case it
is not a delusion—but the truth.

CELADINE: You attempt to flatter me out of my senses.
But you will not. You are a sweet man. For a stranger.

ELLIOT: I am not a stranger.

CELADINE: You think you know me?

ELLIOT: I know your writing.

CELADINE: I am not my writing.

ELLIOT: Everything contained within what you write
must be contained within you. Is that not simple logic?

CELADINE: Simple and skewed, yes.

ELLIOT: If you could only reach inside.

CELADINE: "Inside," you say?

ELLIOT: Yes. It seems to me, if I may be so bold—

CELADINE: —why stop now?

ELLIOT: Your work suffers from your having no real
regard for it yourself. You especially seem to avoid the
workings of the heart. You should write more of what
you feel, rather than only what you know. You should
write what you do *not* know—and you should write
especially—what you are *afraid* to feel.

CELADINE: And so now the stranger is a critic.

ELLIOT: No. I am but a lowly actor. I know my station in
life. But I also know when I see a comet streaking across

the sky. You will forgive me for wanting to hang on to its tail—even if only for a brief instant.

CELADINE: Comets are fleeting.

ELLIOT: As are we all.

CELADINE: If I ever did write another play it would be my last.

ELLIOT: Then such would be the worlds' loss.

CELADINE: You are a very smooth talker. For such a— young man.

ELLIOT: Not so young as you.

CELADINE: And not such a bad liar, either.

(Pause)

ELLIOT: I have been in your company before.

CELADINE: Have you?

ELLIOT: Yes, there is no reason you should remember. I was-

CELADINE: —"but a boy?"

ELLIOT: No, not "but a boy." A young man in fact.

CELADINE: As opposed to now, you mean?

ELLIOT: I confess to being a bit hesitant to bring this up with you. Perhaps I should not.

CELADINE: I insist.

ELLIOT: It was during rehearsals for your first play; *The Witches Banquet.*

CELADINE: Ah yes,— quite a success by my standards. Running all of a night and a half as it did.

ELLIOT: It was a success to me. A grand success in fact. I thought it was superlative. I was an apprentice at the theatre. I worked in the shop where the sets were built.

And I used to watch you, from the second tier up. I would see you in back, in the corner, always scribbling, with your blonde locks falling over your face and your lips in perpetual motion as you acted out every word of the play to yourself—even as you were writing it.

CELADINE: Yes—it is the only time we playwrights get to hear it done correctly.

ELLIOT: You seemed to me—on fire with inspiration.

CELADINE: Perhaps I was. Then. But that was a long time ago.

(Pause)

ELLIOT: I only ask that you consider what I propose seriously. Perhaps there is another play in you yet.

CELADINE: And what would be my subject?

ELLIOT: Whatever you like. Just do not write about marriage. Miss Behn seems to have—

CELADINE: —Mister Blakely. IF you ever come to know me further—you will know NEVER to mention that name in this house again.

ELLIOT: I am sorry. After all, she is not half the writer you are. Besides, material success is not everything. *(He starts for the door, then turns.)* Though on second thought, perhaps it is. *(He smiles, then starts for the door again.)*

CELADINE: Thank you for coming. You have revived me. Somewhat.

ELLIOT: You can thank me best by putting quill to paper. Goodnight, Celadine.

(He bows, kisses her hand, then walks out. CELADINE stands frozen as the lights fade.)

(Lights up again the next day. JEFFREY *is standing in the middle of the room, wearing one of* MARY's *dresses. She commands him.)*

MARY: Aaaaand—walk!

(He walks in front of her.)

MARY: Now, with a little sway, like a woman might.

(He walks how he thinks a "woman might".)

MARY: There, do you see how the back bunches up?

(He tries to look behind himself, but keeps going in circles.)

MARY: Stop! You are like a dog, chasing its tail.
Walk again. This time with an "elegant" air.

(He walks "elegantly" across the room.)

MARY: There, see? It needs to be taken in more here.
Can you tailor that for me?

(He shakes "yes".)

MARY: Our good King Charles is having a procession
today. I want to look my best for him. He has been
known, when passing, to look in my general direction.

*(*JEFFREY *nods, suitably impressed.* MARY *starts into the kitchen.)*

MARY: Very well, then—off to work.

*(*JEFFREY *makes a sound with his throat, to get her attention. She turns.)*

MARY: What is it?

*(*JEFFREY *thinks how to express it, then points upstairs.)*

MARY: Upstairs?

(He shakes yes.)

MARY: What upstairs?

(He imitates a woman walking, again.)

MARY: Celadine?

(He shakes yes, excitedly.)

MARY: What of her?

(He imitates someone writing something.)

MARY: Yes, I heard it as well. She was writing again.

(He jumps up and down, clapping.)

MARY: It is a good thing, yes!

(She starts to leave again. He again makes a noise with his throat. She turns back.)

MARY: What is it?

(He points directly at her.)

MARY: Myself?

(He nods yes, then points upstairs again, walks a little again.)

MARY: And Celadine—

(He nods yes, claps.)

MARY: What of us?

(He thinks a moment, then walks to her, points toward her chest.)

MARY: My—bosom?

(He shakes no, points again toward her chest.)

MARY: My heart?

(He shakes yes, then points again toward her heart, and then slowly directs his finger upstairs, in the direction of CELADINE'S *room.)*

MARY: And—Celadine's?

(He shakes yes, then connects two fingers.)

MARY: But of course.

(He suddenly grabs a piece of charcoal off the table, draws a huge letter on the floor with it. MARY looks down at it.)

MARY: "Y?"

(He shakes yes.)

MARY: "Y?" Oh, "why?"

(He shakes yes, then quickly pulls over a small stool and sits on it in front of her.)

MARY: Have you ever been in love?

(He shyly nods yes.)

MARY: Was it returned?

(He sadly nods no.)

MARY: Then you and I have something in common. Why was *your* love not reciprocated?

(He points to his mouth.)

MARY: You cannot speak.

(He nods yes, then suddenly stands, pulling out the linings of both his pockets.)

MARY: And are not rich.

(He nods yes, sits down again.)

MARY: Women of true intelligence would have found those your most desirable attributes.

*(He points upstairs again. Then back to her chest.
Then points to the 'y')*

MARY: I was a whore. In my other life. You know what a "whore" is, do you not?

(He nods yes)

MARY: I was ten when me mother and father started me in it.

(He covers his ears.)

MARY: Oh, but there is no use covering your ears.
It is a fact. *(She holds up her hand)* As this is my hand.
That is a fact. *(She points to a place near her neck.)*
Do you see me pretty scar?

(He nods yes.)

MARY: This my sweet is courtesy of a good fat
Alderman and his happy eight inch blade. Sometimes
the men would take you rough. Oh, and this one had
his fill of me—then went ahead and cut me throat for
good measure.

(JEFFREY has covered his ears again. She approaches him.)

MARY: Oh, do not despair dear child. That is only
a single side of human nature. I have it upon good
authority there are one or two others. *(Pause)* That is
when I first looked upon her face. She came as a savior
to me—lying as I was, in a heap, in the gutter. Me most
awful hour. Everyone walking by—like I was so much
trash. "The dirty whore—got what she deserved,"
they'd say. Some of them spittin' on me. But then
Celadine—I shall never forget—pushing her way past
them all—the gawkers and the awful crowd of animals
they were: "What's a fine lady like that giving a rat's
ass for a rancid whore?"—they'd say. And down she
knelt—beside me. And with a powder blue glove—
she pushed aside me blood soaked hair. And it was
then that I first saw her face. I thought it was the sun,
at first, but it was not. It was she that saved me. Oh,
she is the world to me. And her sweet daughter—
she was the moon. I loved her as me own. And there
are ways that I love Celi—that I know can never be
returned. But, you know what our turgid little friends
the French say: " There is one who kisses—and one
who offers the cheek."

(CELADINE appears at the top of the stairs.)

CELADINE: You are not boring our horse with old stories are you?

MARY: I am not.

CELADINE: And why pray tell, is he wearing a dress?

MARY: He is me model.

CELADINE: I warrant he makes a much prettier horse than he does a woman.

MARY: Aye, I must say he had no complaint putting it on. Methinks he rather likes dressing up as a woman. Do you not, boy?

(JEFFREY *smiles, agreeing. He twirls once in the dress.*)

MARY: That will be enough of that. Go cut wood.

(JEFFREY *starts out the door*)

CELADINE: Though, you may want to take off the dress first. The neighbors have enough to talk about.

(He stops, smiles sheepishly and heads up the stairs, careful not to trip on the dress. When he is up, MARY *turns to* CELADINE.)

MARY: And you.

CELADINE: What of me?

MARY: Ever since that actor came, you have color in your face.

CELADINE: It is not color, it is age.

MARY: He is not an entirely disagreeable sort. That actor.

CELADINE: For an actor, no. But then, there is great relativity in that statement.

MARY: You should eat.

CELADINE: I have no appetite.

MARY: Then you should sleep.

CELADINE: Who will you fuss over when I am gone?

MARY: Where do you plan on going?

(CELADINE does not look at her. MARY walks over to her, starts to brush her hair.)

MARY: When you are an old woman, you are going to have long white hair with curls all the way down to your big fat arse. And you are going to sit on the front stoop of the house—and you are going to rock back and forth on the chair and you are going to complain about the world all the live long day— just as you do now.

CELADINE: And what of Jeffrey? Will we still have him?

MARY: Heaven's no. We will have traded him in for a more youthful model. Just as men are wont to do!

(CELADINE laughs.)

MARY: I could not help but hear the sound of your scratching quill last night. And notice your candle burning until the wee hours.

CELADINE: Accounting chores. I am trying to keep us out of the poor house.

MARY: I heard the speed of your pen. Methinks you are coming alive again as a writer. Why do you not admit it?

CELADINE: An actor suddenly appearing and having a little interest in my work is hardly sufficient to alter my disposition. People cannot save one another, Mary. That is a concept you have trouble comprehending.

MARY: We are not islands.

CELADINE: Some of us however, are.

MARY: You still have your beauty and can command a man's attention. You should allow yourself to be pursued.

CELADINE: Women who expect men to save them are doomed. They are nothing but little girls masquerading as full grown women. They make me sick and besmirch our entire gender.

MARY: You are a stubborn mule.

(A knock at the door. MARY *opens it.* ROWLEY *walks in, carrying a large bag over his shoulder.)*

MARY: Oh, it is only that Rowley.

ROWLEY: Do try to contain your enthusiasm.

CELADINE: Oh, good Rowley. Mary and I were just talking about men.

ROWLEY: Really? Something salacious and profane I hope?

MARY: We agree they are the weaker sex.

ROWLEY: Oh, of that there is no doubt. We are pigs, to be sure.

MARY: Pigs are loyal.

ROWLEY: Then we are French pigs.

CELADINE: Pray, Rowley, are you truthful with the fairer sex?

ROWLEY: Yes, in that I am truthful about the extent to which I am not.

CELADINE: And how is that?

ROWLEY: Well, I say something to them they know is a lie—then they respond in turn with something I am assured is untrue—then the both of us agree to call it "love". Pray, is that not being "truthful" in today's context?

CELADINE: Perhaps, but it is also cynical.

ROWLEY: I would be more sentimental, but I am making the assumption you are both too intelligent to stomach it.

MARY: And I suppose you have had your share of women, eh?

ROWLEY: I would say I have not done badly.

MARY: Funny, you do not strike me as a "rogue."

CELADINE: Oh, Mary, do not let appearances fool you. Mister Rowley is known in some quarters as "Master of the Backstairs."

MARY: You will forgive me if I find that hard to believe.

ROWLEY: Well, then Mary. Perhaps you will allow me to *convince* you of it sometime—over and over and over again. In private quarters, perhaps?

MARY: I would like that. If I were insane.

ROWLEY: Your contempt for me only fuels me interest.

MARY: Your interest in me only fuels me contempt.

ROWLEY: Oh, saucy! Saucy! It has been so long since I have been rejected, I have almost forgotten the sheer thrill of it!

(Suddenly JEFFREY *clomps down the stairs in a horse-like manner. He stops in front of* ROWLEY*)*

CELADINE: This is Jeffrey. Our new—horse.

ROWLEY: I see.

MARY: I must say Rowley—for someone of such modest stature, I do declare you are a conceited man. You should have a good look in a glass sometime and apprise yourself of your own appearance. The way you talk you would think you were royalty.

ROWLEY: I have been told that in a certain light,
I do fairly resemble our king.

(MARY *laughs*.)

MARY: What, you?!

ROWLEY: Indeed, me. Is that so hard to believe?

MARY: Why no, it would not be if the king were a
balding little sprite.

CELADINE: Tisk, tisk, Mary.

ROWLEY: And you know our king well, do you?

MARY: Our Charles? Why, I have seen him myself
with mine own eyes on numerous occasions.
From a distance, perhaps, but I am well familiar
with his visage. The king is a man's man—and if
the rumors are true, quite the "Nasty Dog" as well.

ROWLEY: The king's shoes for instance. Would they not
approximate my own?

MARY: What, those? Have you gone 'round the bend?
The king would never be caught dead in shoes like that.
I have seen the royal footwear up close. The king wears
only the most handsomely styled shoes with red heels
no less.

(ROWLEY *reaches into his bag, pulls out a glorious pair of
shoes and plunks them on the table*.)

ROWLEY: Like these?

MARY: Why yes, pray, what are you about, possessing
shoes such as those?

(ROWLEY *slips the shoes on*. CELADINE *steps up*.)

CELADINE: But what of poor 'ol Rowley's jacket?

ROWLEY: Yes, would this not be appropriate for our
monarch?

MARY: What, that scrap of cloth? The king is resplendent in his fur lined wraps, trimmed with emeralds.

(CELADINE *pulls a sumptuous robe out of* ROWLEY's *bag, slips it on him.*)

CELADINE: Does it look something like this?

MARY: Why, yes but—aye, you are a strange bird—possessing a wrap so very much like the kings.

(JEFFREY *moves over to* ROWLEY, *astonished at the beautiful handiwork on the robe, touching it.*)

ROWLEY: And what of me hair?

CELADINE: I do declare that I detect a certain resemblance to the locks of our Sovereign.

MARY: "Resemblance?" Are you mad? Our good king has gorgeous black locks and sumptuous curls that cascade down his barrel chest like a waterfall.

(CELADINE *pulls out a black wig, hands it to* ROWLEY. *He puts it on.*)

ROWLEY: Does it "cascade" like this?

MARY: Yes, but—why you are very bold, sir, impersonating the king. There are those that have been hanged for less.

ROWLEY: Though if you would be so kind—might I pursue one more line of inquiry?

MARY: What sort of "inquiry?"

ROWLEY: The king's transportation. Now, the king would never have a worn out old glue horse like the one I rode up on, would he?

(MARY *looks out the window.* CELADINE *tries to contain her laughter.*)

MARY: What, *that* old horse? I have seen the king's carriage. It is led by a team of six Arabians, all gray white. And it sparkles in the sun with white diamonds and a fine oak trim.

ROWLEY: I see. Then tell me—

(He goes to the window, takes out a whistle and blows it loudly.)

ROWLEY: —does it look something like that?

(He subtly motions with his head toward the window as we hear the sound of a six-horse carriage rolling to a stop out front. Mary walks over to the window and looks out, then casually looks back at ROWLEY.*)*

MARY: Yes, that is a fair—

(She stops, looks out the window again. Then back at ROWLEY, *standing adorned in all the king's regalia, seeming to have gained a foot in stature. She looks out the window once more, then at* ROWLEY *again, then faints directly into* JEFFREY's *arms.* CELADINE *looks over to* ROWLEY.*)*

CELADINE: Charles, you are shameless.

CHARLES: What, can a king have no fun at all? Am I not allowed some form of levity?

CELADINE: Jeffrey, look after her.

*(*JEFFREY, *still in awe of the king, nods, picks up* MARY *and makes his way out of the room with her in his arms.* CHARLES *turns to* CELADINE.*)*

CHARLES: And besides —having such mischievous fun together—does that not recall for you the splendid and—singular adventures we used to enjoy at Avonshire?

CELADINE: Avonshire was a very long time ago.

CHARLES: But what of our role playing back then, eh? It was a varied and potent amusement as I think back. I

seem to recall a certain frisky little "Milk Maiden,"
tossed on a bail of hay by a marauding and hungry
"Knight of the Black Forest."

CELADINE: Yes, I might have enjoyed such role playing
myself, if only you had allowed me to play the "Milk
Maiden" once or twice.

CHARLES: You have become domesticated and
conventional. Which of course, only makes you
eminently more corruptible and "ripe for the plucking."

(She sweetly breaks from his grip.)

CELADINE: And you—will never change.

CHARLES: Can we be heard?

CELADINE: Not unless someone is intent on it.

CHARLES: You will go to the northeast edge of Spring
Gardens. Someone will approach you. They will not
speak with you—but they will make it clear who they
are. You are to hand them this: *(He hands her a packet
of papers.)* and you are to pay special attention to
their appearance. You will return and apprise me
of everything that has transpired. That is all.

CELADINE: How perfectly simple.

ROWLEY: Simple, yes. Unless you are found out and
tortured to death. You should regard yourself from
this moment onward, as being in hourly danger.

CELADINE: And if I *am* killed?

ROWLEY: Our agreement stands. You have my word.
(He opens the door.) God speed, Celadine. *(He starts to
leave, then turns back.)* Oh, and tell our good Mary not
to wait up for me, will you?

*(He smiles, then walks out the door. We hear royal fanfare in
the distance, then music of the period softly as* CELADINE

walks over to the last candle in the room. She lingers over it a moment, then blows it into darkness.)

END OF ACT ONE

ACT TWO

(The next day. MARY *stands across from* CELADINE. JEFFREY *sits in the corner)*

MARY: Did it never occur to you to mention, even in passing, that the father of our sweet girl was—The King of England!?

CELADINE: It never did.

MARY: And why is that?

CELADINE: What difference would it have made?

MARY: "What difference"—

CELADINE: —would you have loved her more?

MARY: I could not have loved her more. But all the times he passed by us, in his processions. When he would attend the theatre and walk within inches of us—it never occurred to you to bring it up?

CELADINE: I did not have a child with a king. I had a child with a man I loved—who happened to be king.

MARY: And yet from him, never a penny?

CELADINE: What does he owe me? Why should I be another of his pensioned off mistresses? Their only claim to notoriety is being able to hold their legs up in the air long enough to assure never having to do an honest days work again. I would rather be able to look myself in the glass every morning.

MARY: Then what are you to each other?

CELADINE: We are friends.

MARY: "Friends?" That is all?

CELADINE: I am a busy woman. And as for the king, does he not have enough to distract him? Besides the fact that we are on the verge of war, how many bastard children do you think he has across this isle of his? Hmm? Ten? Twenty? Some say more than a hundred little bastards running about. And mistresses? How many of them? Not to mention that wife. I for one do not depend on other people for my happiness. That is what perpetually unhappy people do.

MARY: And what legacy might our girl have in relation to the king—could you tell me that?

CELADINE: I am in the process of assuring one.

MARY: How exactly?

CELADINE: You need not know everything.

MARY: No, apparently I need not. Indeed, there is clearly quite a bit I do not need to know. But what else might you be kind enough to divulge to me? That you were born on the moon, perhaps? Or that your mother was a six headed cyclops? And your father, was he by any chance, Zeus, God of all creation?

CELADINE: You are full of piss and vinegar today.

MARY: And what of our sweet Jeffrey over there? Perhaps he is the Emperor of China? And you have just neglected to mention it to me.

(JEFFREY, *confused, shakes his head, denying it. A knock at the door.* MARY *opens it in a fit of pique.*)

MARY: What?!

(ELLIOT *steps in, sheets of paper in his hand.*)

ELLIOT: Elliot Blakely at your service.

MARY: Oh, the actor.

ELLIOT: That *is* my profession.

MARY: Or on second thought, perhaps you are not an actor but instead the ghost of Mister William Shakespeare himself. *(At* CELADINE*)* And I have just yet to be informed of it!

CELADINE: That will be all, Mary. Do forgive her Mister Blakely, she is not right today.

MARY: What day am I ever?

CELADINE: *(To* ELLIOT*)* I see you received my pages.

ELLIOT: I have. And I am most anxious to talk with you about them.

*(*CELADINE *looks to* MARY, *then* JEFFREY.*)*

CELADINE: Will you both excuse us?

*(*MARY *turns to* JEFFREY. *She claps her hands.* JEFFREY *instinctively lowers himself.* MARY *hops on his back.)*

MARY: Come Pythagoras! Let us off!

(She slaps JEFFREY *on the backside and he happily gallops through the kitchen door.* ELLIOT *looks after them.)*

ELLIOT: This *is* a very peculiar house.

CELADINE: We are a band of outcasts.

ELLIOT: And I warrant you would have it no other way.

CELADINE: Perhaps.

*(*CELADINE *glances toward the pages in his hand, apprehensive.)*

CELADINE: Do not by the by, feel obligated to spare my feelings.

ELLIOT: Very well. Then I will have no regard for your feelings whatsoever and come straight to the point.

CELADINE: Go on.

ELLIOT: It is— *(He lingers.)*

CELADINE: Yes?

ELLIOT: Astonishing.

CELADINE: In its ineptness, you mean?

ELLIOT: In its scope.

CELADINE: You do not hate it?

ELLIOT: How could I hate the light cast from a burning star?

CELADINE: You set me higher than I am, and are too generous with your praise.

ELLIOT: You are too unwilling to accept it.

CELADINE: There are many things I believe need improving.

ELLIOT: The only thing it needs—is to be finished.

CELADINE: I am still not convinced I am capable.

ELLIOT: With all due respect, milady—that is no longer up to you.

CELADINE: How could that be?

ELLIOT: Because at present—and as it will a thousand years from now, this work belongs to the ages. It already exists: Here.

(He lays his hand on her heart. She freezes.)

ELLIOT: Your only job now, is to allow the rest of it— to unveil itself.

(She moves away from him)

CELADINE: That is much easier said than done. Besides, you should not have praised me so much. Nothing is more damaging to a writer than praise. Should I ever receive any publicly, I will let you know the extent to which I find that true.

ELLIOT: Then let me put your fears to rest and bring up one minor flaw.

CELADINE: I see. Already in the space of ten seconds it has gone from a "perfect" play to a flawed one. I fear if I stand here ten seconds more, it will descend into being a "complete debacle."

ELLIOT: There is only one aspect of it—that for me, does not resonate.

CELADINE: Which?

ELLIOT: The ship wreck. The storm, and the loss of the heirloom. The heirloom is a doll made of porcelain and silk, is it not?

CELADINE: It is. What about that fails to convince you?

ELLIOT: Our heroine is off on a journey, on a ship.

CELADINE: She is.

ELLIOT: Leaving London because of—the plague, is it?

CELADINE: That is correct.

ELLIOT: Yet, she is established earlier as being not well off. Destitute, even. How does she—and her maid servant for that matter, acquire the means to travel?

CELADINE: I leave that unclear.

ELLIOT: You do, yes. That is why I bring it up.

CELADINE: I imagine she is supported by a patron of some influence.

ELLIOT: Yes, you do hint at her having some relation to—a member of the court?

CELADINE: I believe so, yes.

ELLIOT: But who in the court? It is never made clear.

CELADINE: I do not wish to make it clear. I wish to give my audience a modicum of credit.

ELLIOT: Credit for what, the ability to read your mind?

CELADINE: I do not regard my own existence as easily definable. Why should my perception in something I write be any more clear?

ELLIOT: I only raise the issue because I believe it may prove distracting.

CELADINE: I can see why you are such an admirer of—that *other* playwright. Like her, you like your meat served on a platter.

ELLIOT: I see no reason to raise your defenses. I am only making an observation.

CELADINE: Is there anything worse in this world than an actor with "observations"?

ELLIOT: You are a vexing person.

CELADINE: Only in relation to the world I live in. When I am in hell, I expect to be regarded as sublime.

ELLIOT: And so ends my critique.

CELADINE: There was more?

ELLIOT: There was, yes. I see however that you do not possess the constitution to withstand hearing it.

CELADINE: Now I am not only "unclear," but I am "without constitution" as well?

ELLIOT: In this regard I would say you are, yes.

CELADINE: And who are you to speak to me like that?

ELLIOT: No one at all. That is true. I am in the end, just an uncomplicated actor. Perhaps you are correct. I have no right to venture anywhere past the footlights with my silly ideas. Funny is it not, however? No doubt you fashion yourself somewhat of a libertine. Your ideas;

worldly, progressive, dare I say "liberal" even. Except of course when someone disagrees with you, or heaven forbid contradicts you. Then somehow that "open-mindedness" you no doubt take so much pride in—evaporates like so much morning mist. Indeed, Celadine—you are much better off surrounding yourself with people who fawn over your every word. Or, better yet, as in the case of your affectionate "horse-like" friend, are unable to say anything at all. That way, you are always assured of being the greatest wit in every room you inhabit. Should you ever be interested in knowing how you may fare in the *larger* world however, do not hesitate to contact me.*(He leaves the pages.)*Good day.

(He starts out. She calls out to him.)

CELADINE: Stop!

(He does.)

CELADINE: There *is* something worse than an actor making an observation. It is an actor making an observation—that is correct. What else?

(She hands him back the pages. He looks though them.)

ELLIOT: The heirloom—

CELADINE: What of it?

ELLIOT: Your heroine's description of the wreck is horrifying. I feel at once as though I am transported to the event. Can a ship really break in two like that? Like a twig?

CELADINE: I have it on good authority.

ELLIOT: And the rocks, ripping it open. There is sheer terror in it. The irony of course being that they were so close to shore.

CELADINE: Yes, God would seem to have had no lack of humor that day.

ELLIOT: But then, if I am not mistaken, she describes the doll as being hurled overboard. A massive wave comes and takes it all at once.

CELADINE: So I have written, yes.

ELLIOT: She and her maid servant make a heroic attempt to hold onto it. It is just over the side of the ship, caught in the netting, and they are desperately trying to recover it, trying to pull the little doll back on board.

(Beginning here, we start to hear the sound of the storm, the breaking apart of the ship.)

CELADINE: So they were.

ELLIOT: And for a moment it seems as though they will. But then another wave—

(The fury at its loudest, and the distinct scream of a little girl)

ELLIOT: And she is lost.

(CELADINE is frozen, distracted)

ELLIOT: Do you follow?

CELADINE: Go on.

ELLIOT: Until later that day, when the storm has subsided and they find pieces of her—the doll that is— on the shore. How does she describe it?

(He checks the pages, finds one in particular.)

ELLIOT: Yes, here: "In pieces, shattered— And with every new wave, another fragment of her would be laid directly at our feet. As though God were serving her up to us. And mocking us at the same time. And so it was for a full day that we collected pieces of our own heart—and were thankful when the sun finally dropped off—and the gift of darkness descended upon us."

CELADINE: Too flowery, to be sure.

ELLIOT: That is not my criticism of it.

CELADINE: Then what is?

ELLIOT: That what you refer to is merely a doll. Should it not be something more—

(CELADINE looks about to break. He suddenly realizes.)

ELLIOT: Gods Mercy. I *am* a stupid actor. It did not occur to me you wrote from experience.

CELADINE: It is of no consequence.

ELLIOT: Of course it is. I am a fool. I should have—

CELADINE: —I should not have tried to write it.

ELLIOT: That is not true.

CELADINE: No matter, though. It will never be seen. Give it to me.

(She extends her arm for the pages.)

ELLIOT: Celadine—

CELADINE: This instant.

(He hands them to her. He turns and starts to leave, then turns back.)

ELLIOT: One more inquiry, if I may.

CELADINE: What?

ELLIOT: If you are not what you write—what or with whom exactly, am I falling in love with?

CELADINE: If you are falling in love, it is only with an idea of who you think I am. Or worse than that, out of pity.

ELLIOT: Then you will forgive me--as once more I feel compelled to contradict you.

(He kisses her. The kiss lingers, she pulls away.)

CELADINE: You are a foolish actor.

(They kiss again as the lights fade to black. As soon as they do, we hear the sounds of cannon balls exploding. We come up at night. Through the windows of the house we see vague illumination in concert with the sound of the balls landing. As the lights come up fully, we find MARY speaking in the direction of the closet as the explosions continue throughout.)

MARY: Come out, I implore you!

(No movement from the closet)

MARY: Have you no regard for your reputation? *(No movement)* Do you want to be known as a coward? A lily livered pansy boy?!

(Slowly the closet door opens. Out steps JEFFREY, shaking his head "no" in response to the last question. A cannon ball lands a little closer. JEFFREY runs back into the closet without hesitation, slamming the door behind him.)

MARY: You are pathetic! It is only scattered shot, Jeffrey. The Dutch are simply toying with us! It is a tactic meant only to scare the least—"rational" among us.

(After a moment of silence, JEFFREY begins to open the door just a couple inches. Another cannon shot. He slams the door shut immediately.)

MARY: And, of course in your case it is proving extremely effective.

(Now she turns to the door, shouting louder than ever.)

MARY: COME OUT!

(JEFFREY comes out again, cautiously. This time he carries a broom with him, holding it defensively.)

MARY: I see. Somehow you believe that if the house is more "tidy," the Dutch will be mysteriously compelled to cease firing? Is that your plan?

(He shakes "no," then turns the broom handle forward, jabbing at the air in what he would consider "violent" thrusts.)

MARY: Yes, I feel much safer now.

(A knock at the door. JEFFREY quickly runs with the broom back into the closet without hesitation, slamming the door behind him. MARY speaks directly to it.)

MARY: No, let me. *(She moves to the door, calls through it.)* Pray, who knocks? Are you Dutch?

(A familiar voice)

VOICE: If I am Dutch, you are not English.

(MARY hastily pulls open the door. CHARLES, in the guise of "Rowley," steps quickly inside.)

MARY: Oh, Milord! *(She drops to her knees)*

ROWLEY: Oh no no—none of that, please. I am—

MARY: —me Liege, me Most Beneficent of Monarchs!

ROWLEY: No, no, do get up! Get up! There really is no time for this. I implore you—

MARY: *(Extending her hand)* Oh, but for The Kings' touch!

ROWLEY: Please, do stop!

MARY: YOU are a father to *all* your people.

ROWLEY: A great many perhaps, but "all" may be straining the limits of credulity.

MARY: —how may I be of service?

ROWLEY: By getting off your knees. I beg of you!

(She gets up.)

ROWLEY: That is much more to my liking, thank you.

(Suddenly the closet door opens, JEFFREY *starts out.*
ROWLEY *instinctively pulls out his dagger, pointing*
it straight at him.)

ROWLEY: Who goes!?

*(*JEFFREY, *horrified, turns around and runs into the closet*
again, slamming the door.)

ROWLEY: *(Replacing his dagger)* Yes, no doubt with
staunch defenders of the crown such as that, we will
have no trouble repelling the Dutch. Where is Celadine?

MARY: Oh, me Sovereign! Me most—

ROWLEY: Ah ah ah!

MARY: Forgive me. My friend slipped out unannounced
and has yet to return. Have we reason to fear for her
safety?

ROWLEY: I am hoping not.

(We hear a volley of cannon balls landing as CELADINE
suddenly rushes through the door, out of breath. She wears
a hood, throwing it off her head. MARY *rushes forward.)*

MARY: Celi!

CELADINE: I am well. Do not concern yourself.

(She turns, notices ROWLEY *there.)*

CELADINE: We have much to discuss.

ROWLEY: No doubt.

*(*CELADINE *turns to* MARY.*)*

CELADINE: Allow me to speak with his majesty in
confidence.

MARY: Of course. *(She goes to the closet, knocks on the*
door.) Come out brave Lancelot!

*(*JEFFREY *cautiously steps out)*

MARY: You can hide under your bed.

(MARY *takes him by the hand. Another series of explosions are heard as* JEFFREY *dashes upstairs ahead of* MARY *as she shakes her head in disgust, following him. From this point on we hear the explosions at greater intervals and from a greater distance.* ROWLEY *faces* CELADINE.)

ROWLEY: What news?

(CELADINE *holds up the folded packet.*)

ROWLEY: It remains undelivered. Tell me why.

CELADINE: I waited exactly where I was told. It had grown entirely dark except for the blue moon.

ROWLEY: And no one came?

CELADINE: No, someone did. I saw his—or her— silhouette coming out from the trees on the edge of Spring Gardens. Whomever it was, came closer, taking measured steps straight toward me. Then suddenly, the shadowy figure stopped. As though unsure whether to come nearer. I took down my hood in order that I might be able to nod some signal of assurance, that yes, it was safe to advance. Then suddenly the apparition vanished, disappearing straight into a line of trees. Then nothing, not even a sound.

ROWLEY: This is not happy news.

CELADINE: What else could I have done?

ROWLEY: It confirms my suspicions.

CELADINE: And those are?

ROWLEY: That you are known to this "apparition." To this filthy traitor.

CELADINE: That I "am known?" Make clearer your meaning.

ROWLEY: He did not advance, because he knew you would recognize him. He saw your face, though you did not see his. I placed you there to test this theory.

CELADINE: "Placed" me?

ROWLEY: My spies have had suspicions about this traitor for some time.

CELADINE: And who exactly do you—

ROWLEY: —Elliot Blakely, your "actor."

CELADINE: That is preposterous.

ROWLEY: Is it really? Just showed up one day for a "play," did he? Rather an admirer of your writing, is he? He knows of our union and of our history together. He is using you to get to me. He is a Protestant zealot, working for the Dutch. He is convinced I am a Catholic in sheep's clothing.

CELADINE: But is that not true?

ROWLEY: The extent to which it happens to be true is most assuredly beside the point.

CELADINE: The insular life you lead has given rise to unfounded suspicion. Now you see shadows around corners where even the corners do not exist.

ROWLEY: You are enamored of him. The man has designs to kill me, and you remain "a flutter."

CELADINE: And you are jealous.

ROWLEY: "Jealous?" Jealous of what? A third rate actor and a second rate spy? I have seen this man's Hamlet. I should have had him killed for that, let alone the harm he does now.

CELADINE: You cut a sorry figure.

ROWLEY: I plan on killing this creature before he kills me. That after all, is the prerogative of kings. To that end, I command you to find a pretense for us to meet tomorrow. Let him know I will attend, either as Rowley or as the king. It makes no difference now, as he most assuredly knows me as both. But by this time tomorrow, I will have my satisfaction.

CELADINE: How exactly?

ROWLEY: My spies have informed me that his intended method is poison. I will hoist him on his own petard.

CELADINE: In truth, are you certain you are an important enough monarch to kill?

ROWLEY: If I am wrong, he will acquit himself and our meeting will come to nothing. But if I am right. Well, I am always right, so there is no point in even discussing it further.

CELADINE: And so I was nothing but a pawn?

ROWLEY: On a more celestial level; are not we all? *(He starts for the door.)*

CELADINE: And what of our agreement?

(He stops, turns.)

ROWLEY: When your work is done—she will have a last name.

(From this point on, the sound of cannon shot is no longer heard. Just as ROWLEY starts to open the door, ELLIOT rushes through it. ROWLEY and he are face to face.)

ELLIOT: I do beg your pardon.

ROWLEY: *(Under his breath)* No doubt you will.

(ELLIOT turns to CELADINE.)

ELLIOT: I was anxious to see if you came to any harm.

CELADINE: I thank you for your concern. Elliot; Mister Rowley. Mister Rowley, Elliot Blakely.

ROWLEY: The thespian, Elliot Blakely?

ELLIOT: Yes. Are you familiar with my work?

ROWLEY: More than you could ever know.

ELLIOT: I am flattered. Are you yourself associated with the theatrical arts?

ROWLEY: Moi?

ELLIOT: Yes, you.

ROWLEY: Well, I suppose in some respects I am an "actor."

ELLIOT: In what respect is that?

ROWLEY: In that I do sometimes play the fool. But mark me, I only "play" at it while others seem intent on making it their vocation.

ELLIOT: Alas, I myself have never played the fool.

ROWLEY: Not that you have been aware of, you mean?

ELLIOT: The essence of your meaning evades me.

ROWLEY: Oh, while I do find this slightly diverting "thrust and parry" entertaining, alas, I must take my leave. *(Turns to* CELADINE*)* Goodnight, sweet lady. *(Back to* ELLIOT*)* A pleasure—Mister Blakely.

ELLIOT: Mine entirely—Mister Rowley.

*(*ROWLEY *smiles conspicuously toward* CELADINE, *then leaves.* ELLIOT *faces her.)*

ELLIOT: He is a bit of an odd fellow. Old friend?

CELADINE: I did think so. Now truth be told, I am not sure *who* my friends are.

ELLIOT: How could you say that?

CELADINE: Where were you tonight?

ELLIOT: Everywhere it seems. It has been an eventful day, has it not?

CELADINE: For some more than others, I suppose.

ELLIOT: There is good news: The Dutch look as though they will be repelled.

CELADINE: You have that on good authority, do you?

ELLIOT: I need no more authority than my own eyes. The king will prevail.

CELADINE: Tell me; are you an admirer of his?

ELLIOT: The king?

CELADINE: Yes.

ELLIOT: How could I not be? What with all he has done for our profession.

CELADINE: He does like a good drama.

ELLIOT: I have always thought him partial to comedy.

CELADINE: You will forgive me if I get the two confused lately. So often in life I find they—intermingle so.

ELLIOT: Yes, I suppose you are right. Speaking of which, have you had a chance to finish your own?

CELADINE: Do you mean the drama I was writing or the one in which I live?

ELLIOT: Either, I suppose.

CELADINE: Are you my friend, Elliot?

ELLIOT: How could you ask that?

CELADINE: Answer me directly.

ELLIOT: Has something changed between us?

CELADINE: That is what I am trying to ascertain. Are you my friend?

ELLIOT: Of course I am.

CELADINE: If you are not—

ELLIOT: —what exactly is...

CELADINE: —HEAR ME! If you are not my friend, and you are taking me for a fool—you must leave and find

yourself on the next boat that crosses water.
Do you understand that?

ELLIOT: What is this madness? Where is the friend
I know?

(He tries to move toward her, she moves away.)

CELADINE: The friend you know is providing you a way
out. If you are a liar, be clear: you are in peril.

ELLIOT: You might as well be speaking in a foreign
tongue.

CELADINE: This is a precarious world and I am clinging
to it by a thread.

(He moves to her again.)

ELLIOT: Then allow me to hold you.

(She moves away.)

CELADINE: I have other concerns. Neptune caught her.
Escorting her down to the silent depths all by himself.
And everyday, he and his menagerie of mermaids see
to it that her golden hair is brushed.

ELLIOT: Celadine—

CELADINE: And that her dress—

ELLIOT: —Are you not aware of yourself?

CELADINE: —He is fair and good. And at the appointed
hour he will release her and when he does—

(He grabs her by the shoulders, Hard.)

ELLIOT: —CELADINE! *Your thoughts are not your own!*

(She tries to recognize him again.)

CELADINE: Who are you?

ELLIOT: It is Elliot.

CELADINE: And you are—who you say you are?

ELLIOT: Of course I am.

CELADINE: And you are my friend?

ELLIOT: More than that.

(He holds her tightly. She seems greatly relieved. Slowly, she breaks away.)

CELADINE: I should rest.

ELLIOT: It has been an exhausting day.

CELADINE: I must sleep.

ELLIOT: Of course. Can I help you—

CELADINE: —no. We will see each other tomorrow, then?

ELLIOT: I would like that. Perhaps a party—to celebrate the king's victory.

CELADINE: If you would like.

ELLIOT: After you have had your rest.

CELADINE: Mid-afternoon, then?

ELLIOT: Mid-afternoon. Sweet dreams, Celadine.

(He gets on one knee, kisses her hand and starts out. Suddenly, he turns back.)

ELLIOT: Oh. And do invite that "Rowley."

(She stops climbing the stairs, looks straight back at him.)

CELADINE: Why?

ELLIOT: No particular reason. He seems a colorful sort is all.

CELADINE: I will do what I can.

ELLIOT: Perfection. Goodnight again, my sweet.

(He opens the door and leaves)

CELADINE: Goodnight.

(CELADINE *stands frozen on the stairs as the lights fade slowly to black. As soon as they do, we hear church bells ringing all around London, declaring victory as the lights come up the following day. Standing on the stairs is* JEFFREY. *He is holding a basket filled with flower petals and throwing them liberally down to the main room. The petals cascade beautifully downward as* MARY *steps out of the kitchen and notices them all around her. As the bells stop ringing,* MARY *looks up and sees* JEFFREY *with a huge smile on his face. She yells up at him.*)

MARY: You doxy! Those are for his majesty!

(*Oblivious, he continues to throw them down on her.*)

MARY: Stop wasting them!

(*He stops.* MARY *shakes her head.*)

MARY: Why do I even bother? The youth of today are hopeless. They have the mental faculties of cheese.

(*Knock at the door.* MARY *jumps.*)

MARY: It is him!

(*She looks up at* JEFFREY.)

MARY: Come! Stand as we rehearsed!

(JEFFREY, *excited, runs down and sets himself in front of the door. He stands at awkward attention, then proceeds to bow in a ridiculously exaggerated manner.*)

MARY: Not yet you bag of sand! Wait until I open the door!

(JEFFREY *nods, embarrassed. He sets himself again. More knocks.* MARY *spits on her hand, straightens her hair, then ceremoniously opens the door as* JEFFREY *begins another ridiculous bow.*)

MARY: Your most gracious—

(ELLIOT *steps through the door with a walking stick.*
MARY's *face falls.*)

MARY: —oh, the actor.

(JEFFREY, *recovering from his "bow," looks up in obvious
disappointment*)

ELLIOT: I see my presence under-whelms you both.
You are expecting someone of consequence?

MARY: Only he that is most consequential. A dear
friend of ours in fact.

ELLIOT: Really?

MARY: Oh yes, I have known him for some time now.
Of course I did not know that I knew him, but now that
I know that I did, it will be known to everyone who did
not know—that I did know that—I—or, something
along those lines.

(JEFFREY *is confused, as is* ELLIOT.)

ELLIOT: I—see. Where is Celadine?

MARY: She is dressing.

(*The sound of horses and a carriage outside*)

ELLIOT: Who comes?

(MARY *looks out the window.*)

MARY: It is the King's carriage. He is arrived! Places!
Take your places!

(JEFFREY *grabs the basket of petals, takes his place once again
in front of the door, ready to bow.* ELLIOT *moves off to the
side. Suddenly a fanfare is heard.* MARY *almost swoons.*)

MARY: Oh, he honors us! Everyone in London will see.

(*More fanfare, then a short knock at the door*)

MARY: Yes! I am coming, me Celestial. Me...

(*A familiar voice through the door*)

VOICE: Dispense with the cow dung and open the door!

(Another longer fanfare as MARY *quickly opens the door. Stepping through it is* CHARLES, *entirely dressed as the king, resplendent. He turns back toward the horn blowers.)*

CHARLES: Will you STOP that blaring!?

(The fanfare comes to a bedraggled end,)

CHARLES: Have you no regard for my ears!? How many times must I remind you?!

*(*CHARLES *slams the door, mumbling under his breath.)*

CHARLES: Coxcombs.

(He turns around, sees ELLIOT *and* MARY *on their knees.* JEFFREY *finishes his peculiar bow.)*

CHARLES: Lovely, from a street full of ass smoochers to a room full of them. Story of my life. Do get up.

(They all do.)

MARY: *(To* JEFFREY*)* Oh, the petals! The petals, you stupid cow!

*(*JEFFREY *suddenly remembers, then begins to skip around the king, reaching into the basket and going through the motion of tossing the flower petals into the air. Only, there are no more petals. Still, he continues to skip around all three of them, tossing invisible petals and smiling obliviously. This goes on for an uncomfortable amount of time with everyone looking on in disbelief. Then)*

CHARLES: Would someone be kind enough to inform me—am I in hell?

*(*MARY *slaps* JEFFREY *on the back of the head. He stops skipping. She looks to* CHARLES.*)*

MARY: Do forgive us sire. We ran out of petals.

CHARLES: You are forgiven. *(Looks to* ELLIOT*)* Mister Blakely is it?

ELLIOT: Your Majesty. An honor.

CHARLES: Yes, one you have had before. Are you aware?

ELLIOT: That has just occurred to me this very moment, sire.

CHARLES: Has it?

ELLIOT: Had I only known—

CHARLES: Yes, I have heard that before.

(Turns to MARY)

CHARLES: Where is my friend?

(CELADINE enters on the stairs)

CELADINE: Your friend is late—as usual.

(They all turn and look up at her. She is wearing a most exquisite, almost breath taking dress)

CELADINE: And asks your forgiveness.

CHARLES: I can assure you—you have mine. As to theirs; what does it matter, since, as has already been noted—you have mine.

CELADINE: You are so much nicer when you are "Rowley."

CHARLES: It is the clothes. You cannot help but be an obnoxious fop when you are dressed up in this— puffery. That is the dress I had made for you)is it not?

CELADINE: You have always been most generous, Your Majesty.

(ELLIOT steps up, looks to CELADINE.)

ELLIOT: You are glowing.

CELADINE: And you —are too kind.

CHARLES: "Glowing" is fine. I myself would have described her apparition as a "portal to the heavens." "A myriad of—"

CELADINE: —I do get the point, your Majesty.

(MARY *clears her throat, then*)

MARY: I too— am wearing a dress.

(ELLIOT *and* CHARLES *chime in at once.*)

ELLIOT: CHARLES:
Oh yes, very nice.   Charming.

CELADINE: It is you who are the true vision, dear Mary. I have looks that require adornment—you have the sort of timeless beauty that requires none.

(MARY *blushes, curtsies toward* CELADINE.)

CHARLES: Well, let us begin our revelry. To celebrate our recent victory and to toast the long life of our beloved England.

MARY: Here, here, oh, Person of Quality!

CHARLES: Keeper of the house: Have you a suitable refreshment?

MARY: I do sire, if you will allow. A simple port.

CHARLES: Fetch it.

MARY: Yes, good king.

(*She bows, backs out into the kitchen along with* JEFFREY. CELADINE *walks downstairs.* CHARLES *turns to* ELLIOT.)

CHARLES: Mister Blakely.

ELLIOT: Sire?

CHARLES: When may we have the honor of seeing you onstage in future?

ELLIOT: I currently have no set plans, Your Highness.

CHARLES: Ah yes, the life of an actor. "Between engagements," are we?

ELLIOT: It would seem so, Your Majesty.

CHARLES: Yes, not too unlike the life of a monarch. I myself was out of work for some time until this job came up again.

ELLIOT: And England is the better for it, My Sovereign.

CHARLES: Yes, some seem to think so. Unfortunately, some do not. Unlike you poor actors however, I can have my critics killed.

ELLIOT: Yes, sire, as far as I know, no such provision exists in the theatre.

CELADINE: Give me time. I am working on it.

(MARY *and* JEFFREY *enter with a tray of goblets and a bottle. She places them on a table downstage.* ELLIOT *steps forward.*)

ELLIOT: Allow me.

MARY: That is most kind of you.

(CHARLES *looks at* CELADINE.)

CHARLES: Yes, is it not?

(MARY *sets one goblet apart.*)

MARY: I brought this cup out especially for your highness. It is the one that has been washed— most recently.

CHARLES: You are too kind.

MARY: It is the least we can do, your most gracious King.

(*As* MARY *looks toward the king, we see a moment where* ELLIOT *might have dropped something into the king's goblet just before he pours the port into it. He then turns, offering it to the king*)

ELLIOT: Your Majesty.

CHARLES: How—kind of you.

(The king takes the goblet as MARY *sets about filling the other ones. Suddenly* CHARLES *steps toward her.)*

CHARLES: I would like to return the favor.

MARY: But sire...

CHARLES: I do insist.

MARY: Your wish is me command, me Most Nobel, Lordly Liege. Me most Sovereign and Excellent Person!

(She curtsies, hands him the bottle)

CHARLES: Yes, thank you. I cannot help but notice my title grows exponentially whenever you are kind enough to utter it.

MARY: It is me pleasure, Your Majesty. Me Most—

CHARLES: —that will be all, thank you.

*(*CHARLES *pours* ELLIOT's *goblet, then nimbly switches that goblet with his own.* CELADINE *seems to note it.* CHARLES *hands the goblet to* ELLIOT, *who bows politely. The king then quickly pours the other goblets and turns to distribute them.)*

CHARLES: Celadine.

*(*CHARLES *hands* CELADINE *a goblet, then hands out the others. He stops in front of* JEFFREY.*)*

CHARLES: And you boy—have you reached the age of reason?

*(*JEFFREY *shakes "yes," vigorously.)*

CHARLES: Very well.

*(*CHARLES *hands him a goblet, then turns and faces directly across from* ELLIOT. *All the others encircle them as* CHARLES *raises his goblet.)*

CHARLES: Poets above kings!

ALL: *(Repeat back:)* *"Poets above kings!"* Here here...

(Just as everyone raises the goblets to their lips, CELADINE *calls out.)*

CELADINE: STOP!

(They all hold their goblets. MARY *turns to* CELADINE.*)*

MARY: What is it?

CELADINE: I cannot let this go on.

CHARLES: What is your meaning exactly?

CELADINE: Mister Blakely's goblet.

ELLIOT: What of it?

CELADINE: As well as yours, sire.

CHARLES: Yes?

CELADINE: They are: not sufficiently filled.

CHARLES: Mine is plenty full, I can assure you.

ELLIOT: As is mine.

CELADINE: No, I could not have it thus. Give me the goblets. I will make them right.

CHARLES: There really is no need.

ELLIOT: I agree.

CELADINE: I am the hostess, gentlemen. You should comply with my wishes, however eccentric.

*(*JEFFREY *moves over to both of them. Both* ELLIOT *and* CHARLES *hand over their goblets as* JEFFREY *takes them back to the table.* CELADINE *walks to the table and picks up the bottle. She pours a little into each goblet. Then she conspicuously switches the two goblets back and forth several times as though it were a game of Three Card Monty.)*

CELADINE: Oh, silly me. It seems I have mixed up the goblets. Now, which one—dear me, I cannot remember.

(ELLIOT, *nervously steps up.*)

ELLIOT: I—I believe mine was—on the right.

CELADINE: Are you sure, Elliot?

ELLIOT: I—I believe so.

CELADINE: Do you concur, Royal Highness?

CHARLES: No, I- well, yes, I believe he is correct.

CELADINE: Well, it matters not. Here you are.

(She hands them both a goblet. Both ELLIOT and the king are clearly concerned. CELADINE takes her own goblet, raising it up again.)

CELADINE: Now—you were toasting your Highness?

CHARLES: Yes, yes. To whom or what was I toasting exactly?

CELADINE: "Poets." Something to do with "poets," I believe.

CHARLES: Ah yes. Poets. Alright then. To "poets".

(Everyone repeats again.)

ALL: "Poets!"

(Everyone drinks. ELLIOT and CHARLES however, merely raise their goblets to their mouths. CELADINE takes note.)

CELADINE: *(To both)* What is this? You do not drink. Does my wine repulse you both? Shall you not even partake in a single sip?

ELLIOT: I am not thirsty at present.

CHARLES: Nor am I.

CELADINE: I am much offended. I do insist you both take a drink. Now.

CHARLES: My dear lady—

ELLIOT: I mean no personal offense. I simply—

CELADINE: —I insist you both drink NOW! This very instant!

(*Both men tentatively raise their glasses to their mouths, glaring at one another when suddenly, ELLIOT tosses his goblet aside, deftly pulling out a dagger and lunging for the king.*)

ELLIOT: May you and your pope—burn in hell!

(*Just before the dagger lands, JEFFREY jumps in front of the king, protecting him. The dagger lodges deep in JEFFREY's chest as MARY screams out.*)

MARY: Jeffrey!

(*JEFFREY stands stunned, then pulls the dagger out himself, dropping it on the floor. He tries to speak, but of course can not. He collapses on his back. CELADINE and MARY run to him. ELLIOT looks down.*)

ELLIOT: That was not my intention.

CHARLES: Was it not? Well, let me show you mine.

(*CHARLES pulls out his sword, advances on ELLIOT, who pulls a hidden blade out of his walking stick. A swash-buckling fight ensues, ending with the king striking the blade out of ELLIOT's hand. ELLIOT is cornered with the king's sword inches from his neck. Just as it seems as though the king is about to finish him off we hear CELADINE scream.*)

CELADINE: STOP!

(*CHARLES hesitates.*)

CELADINE: It did not puncture his flesh.

CHARLES: How now?

(*CELADINE pulls JEFFREY up in a seated position, then holds open his shirt. Clearly revealed beneath it, is an elaborately tied whale boned corset.*)

MARY: What—is that my corset you have on?

CELADINE: Indeed it is. It was the whale bone inside of it that saved him. It appears our young stallion has a liking not only for wearing your dresses, but your undergarments as well.

MARY: Why, you carcass of pork! Now—get up off the floor and give your Mary a hug—ya pudding brained half wit!

(JEFFREY *bolts up and into* MARY's *arms, still shaken.* MARY *holds onto him tightly, clearly relieved, as the king once again raises his sword to* ELLIOT's *neck.*)

CHARLES: You sir, may prepare for hell.

CELADINE: No! Charles, you will not kill him. Banish him, yes, but give me your word you will not kill him.

CHARLES: That is too much to ask. Besides being a Protestant spy he made an attempt on the life of a king.

CELADINE: Friend—put it down. The affairs of state are minuscule in comparison to the sincere intentions of one heart. This is my heart speaking to you now. Put it down.

(CHARLES *slowly lowers the sword, then to* MARY.)

CHARLES: Keeper of the House, instruct my men to detain Mister Blakely.

MARY: Yes, sire.

(MARY *goes outside.* ELLIOT *walks toward the door, following her. He suddenly stops, turning to* CELADINE.)

ELLIOT: I would like to make it known; not everything I said was a lie.

CELADINE: I will choose to believe you.

(ELLIOT *exits.* MARY *walks back inside. The king looks to* JEFFREY.)

CHARLES: As for you—horse boy. Come hither.

(JEFFREY, *nervous, walks to the king.*)

CHARLES: On your knees, knave.

(JEFFREY *kneels in front of him. The king again takes out his sword.* JEFFREY *thinks he's about to be killed.*)

CHARLES: *(To* CELADINE*)* Has he a family name?

CELADINE: He does not.

CHARLES: It matters little. *(To* JEFFREY*)* Henceforth you shall be known as: Sir Jeffrey—"Gallop."

(The King knights him. MARY *looks on, speechless.)*

CHARLES: You are also now owner of ten thousand acres of prime farming land to the north.

(MARY *squeals with delight.)*

CHARLES: That is one acre for saving my life—which is approximately what it is worth—and nine thousand nine hundred and ninety-nine acres for having a curious mixture of perversity and foresight to wear a bustier under your shirt. That is representative of the spirit of "good fun" that I hope to encourage more of in my subjects.

MARY: You are most generous, great king.

CHARLES: *(To* JEFFREY*)* It will no longer be of any consequence that you cannot speak. Your money and title will henceforth speak for you.

CELADINE: *(To* CHARLES*)* I recall plainly now— what it was I first saw in you.

CHARLES: Hmmm. Do you really? And as for what I offered you in return for your services. I will keep that promise. Consider that she is now resurrected. At least in name. Lady Margaret of Avonshire.

(CELADINE *bows.)*

CELADINE: You are a man of your word, sire.

(The king moves toward the door, suddenly turning back around.)

CHARLES: It is regretful however; You were correct about that. I do not recall her enough. Our little Margaret. Though there were times—while she lived, when I would watch her from a distance—across a park perhaps or when you took her out boating. You never knew of course. I did not want to create a "commotion" as it were. I remember once in Saint James, when I saw both of you with her. She was running, playing, with some manner of hoop and a stick. And as I do recall there was a magic about her. *(Motioning near his head with his finger)* Was there not a particular quality to the curl of her hair? And when she would— *(He suddenly stops himself.)* But then—as the world knows—I am not one to become sentimental over such things as that. Hmmph. *(Pause)* I bid you: *adieu.*

(The king exits. There is the start of a fanfare, until we hear the King's voice over it O S:)

CHARLES: STOP THAT THIS INSTANT!

(The fanfare comes to a bedraggled end. MARY looks after the king. Closes the door behind him)

MARY: The whole city will know we are in his favor. This house will come to life once more.

CELADINE: I believe it will.

(Pause. MARY turns to JEFFREY.)

MARY: Come *Sir* Jeffrey! You may now be a gentleman of means, but you can still cut wood.

(JEFFREY nods "yes," then follows MARY, galloping into the kitchen. CELADINE stands alone for a moment as we begin to hear music under, as well as the bells of London once more. CELADINE makes her way over to a trunk, opens it and removes a painting. She regards it, then places the painting

on the mantle. She backs away, keeping her eyes trained on it. It is a painting of an exquisitely beautiful young girl—one that very much resembles her mother. The lights begin to fade until only CELADINE *and the picture are illuminated. Then, finally, the light on* CELADINE *diminishes entirely as only the beautiful face of young Margaret floats in the darkness until that too fades to black.)*

END OF PLAY

www.ingramcontent.com/pod-product-compliance
Lightning Source LLC
Chambersburg PA
CBHW052215090426

42741CB00010B/2546